This devotional belongs to:

_____

Dear Parents,

I'm so excited to introduce Jesus' Pinky Promise, a 30-day devotional designed to help your children grow in their relationship with God. This devotional is more than just a collection of Bible verses and activities; it's a tool to encourage your children to memorize God's promises, learn how to pray, and develop a daily habit of reading the Bible.

Each day, your child will explore a promise from God, and through fun and simple activities such as writing, coloring, and reflecting, they will learn how these promises apply to their lives. The goal is to create a meaningful and memorable experience for both you and your child as you walk together on this journey.

Here's what you can expect in each day's reading:
 • A Promise from God: Each day includes a Bible verse that highlights a promise God has made to His children. These promises are words your child can hold onto and trust.
 • What This Means to Me: A brief prompt encourages your child to reflect on how the promise relates to their own life and how they can see God's faithfulness.
 • Challenge of the Day: A simple activity that helps put the promise into action, teaching your child how to live out their faith each day.
 • A Prayer of Thanks: A short prayer to encourage your child to speak to God and thank Him for His promises.

I hope this devotional becomes a cherished time in your home, as you join your child in exploring God's love and promises. I encourage you to take time to read and pray together each day. By doing this, you're not only teaching your child about God's Word, but you're also building a firm foundation for a lifelong relationship with Him.

Thank you for trusting me to walk alongside you and your family on this spiritual journey. I pray that this devotional will inspire your family to grow closer to God and that your children will carry these promises in their hearts forever.

With love and blessings,
Leslie

Bible verses are taken from NASB 1995/NBLA/and another version

This book is designed to teach biblical principles to children in a clear and practical way. It does not replace personal Bible study under the guidance of an adult.

First edition: 2025
ISBN:979-8-9927393-0-5

Visit our website and download our free eBook
**Legacy of Faith: A Powerful Call to Disciple
the Next Generation**
JESUSPINKYPROMISE.COM

Leslie Torres
Author

Illustrator:
Amanda Middleton
Behance.net/amandamiddleton

If this devotional has been a blessing to your family, we kindly ask you to write a five-star review and share it with others. By doing so, you help us fulfill the Great Commission spreading God's Word and blessing more children with His promises.
Together, we can make a difference!

Follow Jesus' Pinky Promise on Social Media:

Table of Content

Week 1

"I will always forgive you."

Day 1

If we confess our sins, He is faithful and righteous to forgive us our sins and to cleanse us from all unrighteousness.
1 John 1:9

What this means to me?

Jesus forgives us when we ask Him. How does it make you feel to know that He always listens to your prayers and forgives you? Write about a time when you said "I'm sorry" to someone and how it made you feel when they forgave you.

_____

_____

_____

_____

Challenge of the day:

Whenever you feel upset or worried today, stop and pray. Ask Jesus to help you and forgive you for anything you've done wrong. Then say something kind to someone in your family.

Thank you prayer:

Dear Jesus, thank You for always forgiving me and for listening to my prayers. Help me to remember that I can talk to You about anything and that You will always love me no matter what.
Amen.

```
S  C  G  D  G  T  V  K  D  S  F  F
B  E  T  H  L  E  H  E  M  S  G  I
S  G  D  S  H  W  G  H  R  A  T  S
Z  R  F  A  W  O  R  D  F  S  A  F
I  H  W  D  R  S  G  I  Y  R  D  H
O  D  I  G  D  J  D  S  W  G  U  E
N  Y  S  F  V  Q  S  C  R  O  W  N
T  J  D  A  X  W  F  I  A  G  S  H
V  W  O  R  S  H  I  P  H  D  J  S
D  Q  M  I  R  A  C  L  E  S  H  K
F  G  E  J  E  K  H  E  S  Q  N  S
Q  F  I  S  H  E  R  M  A  N  U  F
```

WISDOM   WORSHIP   WORD   ZION   BETHLEHEM

CROWN   DISCIPLE   STAR   MIRACLE   FISHERMAN

"Do not be anxious about anything, but in every situation, by prayer and petition, with thanksgiving, present your requests to God."
Philippians 4:6

"I will always hear when you speak to Me."

What this means to me?

Jesus is always listening when we pray. How does it make you feel to know you can talk to Him about anything? Write about something you would like to tell Jesus today.

_____

_____

_____

Challenge of the day:

Take a moment to pray today. Tell Jesus one thing you're thankful for and one thing you need help with. Then share with a family member something you prayed about.

Thank you prayer:

Dear Jesus, thank You for always listening to me when I pray. Help me to remember that I can talk to You anytime about anything. Thank You for caring about my thoughts and feelings. Amen.

Day 3

"In the shelter of your presence you hide them from all human intrigues; you keep them safe in your dwelling from accusing tongues."
Psalm 31:20

"I will always protect you."

What this means to me?

Jesus promises to protect us and keep us safe. How does it make you feel to know that Jesus is always watching over you? Write about a time when you felt safe because of Jesus's love and care.

_____

_____

_____

Challenge of the day:

Think of a way you can help someone feel safe today. It could be offering kind words, sharing a hug, or praying for them. Take a moment to tell Jesus you trust Him to protect you and your loved ones.

Thank you prayer:

Dear Jesus, thank You for always protecting me and keeping me safe. Help me to trust in Your care and to remember that You are always with me. Thank You for being my shelter and my guide.
Amen.

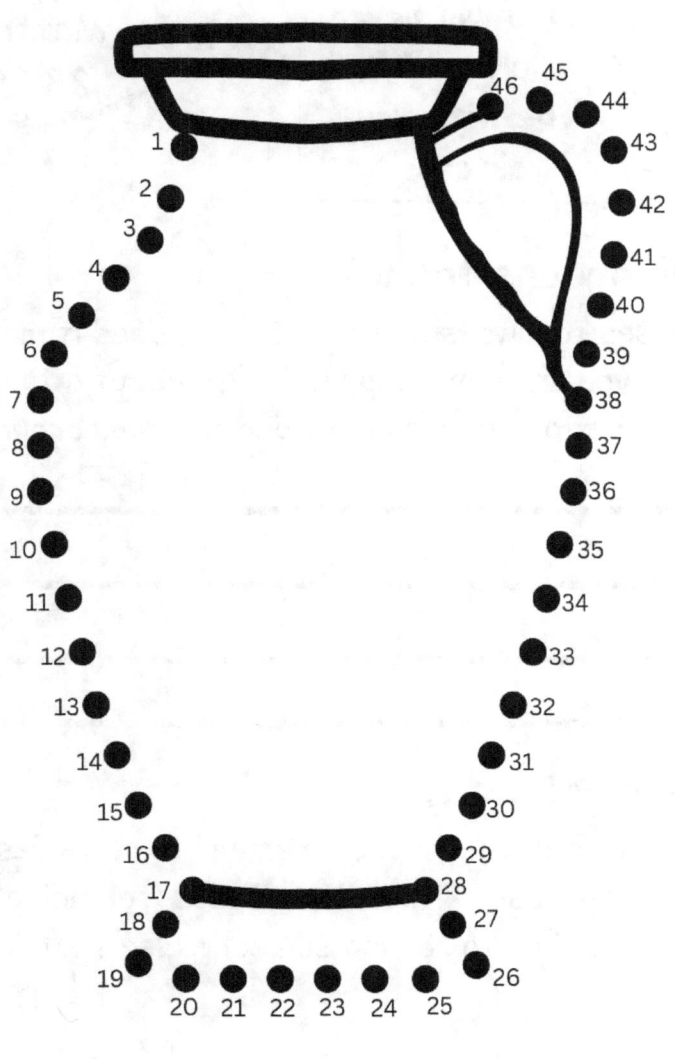

Day 4

"And surely I am with you always, to the very end of the age."
Matthew 28:20b

"You will never be alone; I will be with you always."

What this means to me?

Jesus promises to always be with us. How does it make you feel to know that you are never alone? Write about a time when you felt Jesus close to you, even if no one else was around.

Challenge of the day:

Whenever you feel lonely today, remember that Jesus is always with you. Say out loud, "Thank You, Jesus, for being here with me!" Then, take time to remind someone else that Jesus is with them too.

Thank you prayer:

Dear Jesus, thank You for never leaving me alone. It makes me so happy to know that You are always with me, no matter where I go. Help me to feel Your presence and share Your love with others. Amen.

"I will always counsel you."

Day 5

"I will instruct you and teach you in the way you should go; I will counsel you with my loving eye on you."
Psalm 32:8

What this means to me?

Jesus wants to guide us and help us make good choices. How does it make you feel to know that Jesus is always there to help you? Write about a time when you needed help to decide and how someone helped you.

_____

_____

_____

_____

Challenge of the day:

Think about something you need help with today. Ask Jesus to guide you and give you wisdom to make the right choice. Then, tell someone in your family how Jesus can help us with everything.

Thank you prayer:

Dear Jesus, thank You for always helping me know what to do. I'm thankful that You are always there to guide me and help me make good choices. Please help me follow Your guidance today and always. Amen.

```
N  I  S  C  Y  A  U  Q  V  M  E  L
I  E  H  O  Q  R  T  H  A  N  K  S
E  T  E  M  P  L  E  F  B  S  H  C
J  R  P  V  D  J  X  Z  F  S  B  A
M  U  H  H  X  S  P  I  R  I  T  F
C  V  E  S  R  M  V  C  F  S  E  T
T  I  R  F  A  L  E  A  V  I  N  E
R  M  D  Y  E  U  C  J  I  K  S  V
U  N  E  S  W  A  X  F  R  C  S  B
S  E  B  T  R  U  T  H  T  E  R  T
T  U  K  U  E  Y  B  G  U  X  E  C
W  L  C  A  T  E  N  N  E  W  H  L
```

SHEPHERD	VINE	SPIRIT	TEMPLE	TEN
THANKS	TRUTH	TRUST	VIRTUE	SIN

"I will always strengthen you."

Day 6

"I can do all this through him who gives me strength."
Philippians 4:13

What this means to me?

Jesus gives us strength to keep going, even when things get hard. How does it make you feel to know that with Jesus, you can do anything you need to do? Write about a time when you felt tired or worried, but you were able to do something with Jesus's help.

Challenge of the day:

Today, when you feel tired or discouraged, remember that Jesus gives you strength. Say out loud, "Thank You for giving me strength, Jesus." Then, do something that makes you feel strong and happy.

Thank you prayer:

Dear Jesus, thank You for giving me strength when I feel tired or weak. Help me to remember that with Your help, I can do anything I need to do. Thank You for being my strength and support.
Amen.

Day 7

"Peace I leave with you; my peace I give you. I do not give to you as the world gives. Do not let your hearts be troubled and do not be afraid."
John 14:27

"I will always give you peace."

What this means to me?

Jesus promises to give us peace, even when things feel difficult or scary. How does it make you feel to know that Jesus can give you peace in your heart? Write about a time when you felt worried or afraid but felt peace because of Jesus.

Challenge of the day:

Whenever you feel worried or scared today, take a deep breath, and remember that Jesus gives you peace. Close your eyes and thank Him for the peace He gives you. Share with someone how Jesus can give peace even in hard times.

Thank you prayer:

Dear Jesus, thank You for giving me peace when I feel worried or afraid. Help me to trust in Your peace and remember that You are always with me. Thank You for calming my heart and helping me feel safe.
Amen.

Week 1 Recap

This week, we learned about the promises God has made to us. From His forgiveness to His protection, each promise shows how much He loves and cares for us. We learned
that God is always there to listen, guide, and strengthen us.

Key Takeaways:
  • God promises to always forgive us, no matter what.
  • He hears our prayers and will never leave us.
  • God will protect us and give us peace in every situation.
  • His love is constant, and we can always trust in Him.

Family Activity Idea:
Take some time this weekend to share one of God's promises with your child and pray
together. Remind them that God will always be there, no matter what happens.

Week 2

"Though my father and mother forsake me, the Lord will receive me."
Psalm 27:10

"When you come to Me, I will never reject you."

What this means to me?

Jesus promises that He will never reject us, no matter what. How does it make you feel to know that Jesus always welcomes you with open arms? Write about a time when you felt accepted and loved by someone, and how it made you feel.

Challenge of the day:

Today, remember that Jesus will always accept you, no matter what. Think of someone you can welcome with kindness and love today. Let them know they are accepted and cared for.

Thank you prayer:

Dear Jesus, thank You for always welcoming me and never rejecting me. I am so grateful that You love me no matter what. Help me to always remember that I can come to You with anything, and You will always accept me.
Amen.

```
B E N S X A W Y E B E M
A Q X K U P R A Y E R L
D V E L D T X J R W F O
M F M O S E S B A N E P
I G B U F K Z S M I G E
R Z I D J I E V E S U A
A U I P R O M I S E V C
C T Q I O J D W R E M E
L I D E G N S X E V E R
E P Y C X O U I T N R H
V E P A R A B L E T C B
X S B F E H R S P E Y N
```

MOSES	MERCY	MIRACLE	PROMISE	NOAH
PETER	PEACE	PARABLE	PRAYER	MARY

Day 9

"The Lord is the strength of his people, a fortress of salvation for his anointed one."
Psalm 28:8

"I will always defend you."

What this means to me?

Jesus is our protector and will always defend us from harm.
How does it make you feel to know that Jesus is always there to defend you? Write about a time when you felt protected or safe because of someone's help.

_____

_____

_____

_____

Challenge of the day:

Today, remember that Jesus will always defend you. Think of someone you can defend or protect today. Show them kindness and let them know you care.

Thank you prayer:

Dear Jesus, thank You for always defending me and keeping me safe. I am so thankful that You are my protector. Help me to feel confident knowing You are always there to guard me.
Amen.

Day 10

"As a father has compassion on his children, so the Lord has compassion on those who fear him."
Psalm 103:13

"I will always be compassionate with you."

What this means to me?

Jesus has a loving and compassionate heart for us. How does it make you feel to know that Jesus always cares deeply about you? Write about a time when someone showed you kindness or compassion, and how it made you feel.

_____

_____

_____

_____

Challenge of the day:

Today, think of someone who may need compassion. Show them kindness, whether through a smile, a kind word, or helping them in some way.

Thank you prayer:

Dear Jesus, thank You for always being compassionate with me and showing me Your love. Help me to remember that You care for me deeply. Please help me to show compassion to others just as You do.
Amen.

CONNECT THE DOTS

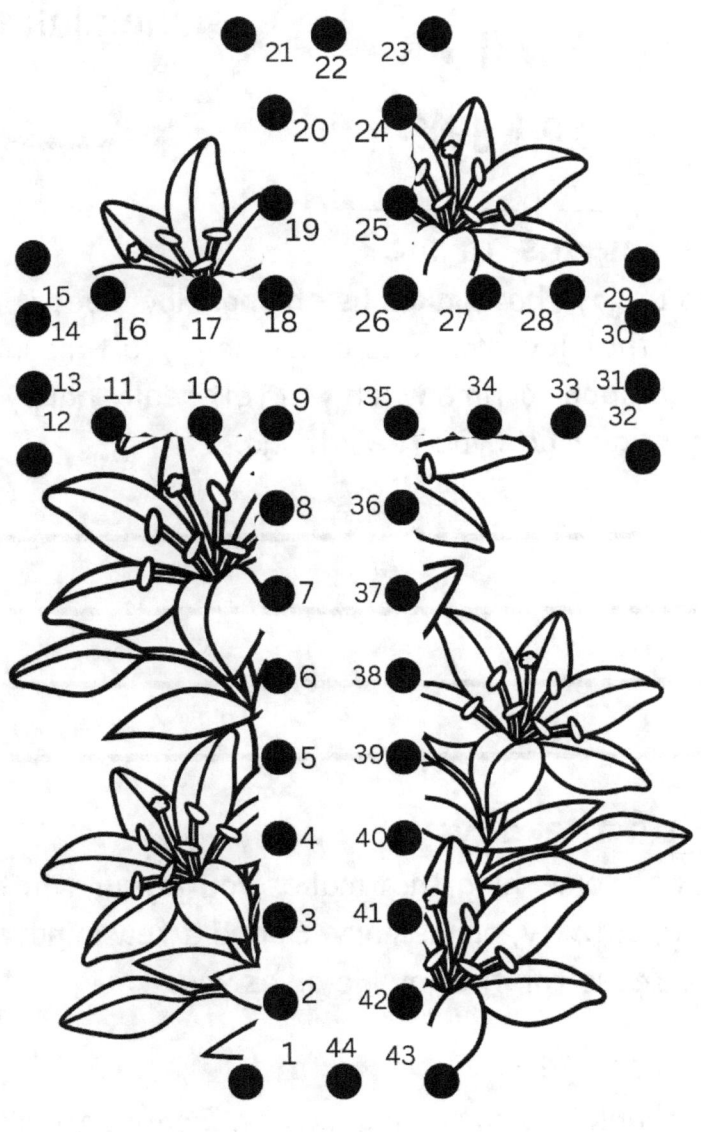

I will give you joy."

Day 11
"The joy of the Lord is your strength."
Nehemiah 8:10b

What this means to me?

Jesus gives us joy that makes us strong. How does it make you feel to know that joy from Jesus can help you through hard times? Write about a time when you felt really happy or joyful, and how that joy made you feel strong.

_____

_____

_____

_____

Challenge of the day:

Today, think of something that makes you joyful, whether it's a favorite song, activity, or memory. Spend a few minutes enjoying it and thank Jesus for the joy He gives you.

Thank you prayer:

Dear Jesus, thank You for giving me joy. I am so thankful that Your joy makes me strong. Please help me to feel Your joy every day, no matter what happens.
Amen.

"My command is this: Love each other as I have loved you."
John 15:12

"I will always love you."

What this means to me?

Jesus loves us with an unchanging love. How does it make you feel to know that Jesus will always love you, no matter what? Write about a time when you felt really loved and how that made you feel.

_____

_____

_____

_____

Challenge of the day:

Today, think of one way you can show love to someone around you whether through a kind word, a small act of kindness, or a smile.

Thank you prayer:

Dear Jesus, thank You for always loving me. I am so grateful for Your constant love. Help me to love others the way You love me. Amen.

```
P  Z  R  I  G  H  T  T  E  O  U  S
E  V  E  A  E  S  P  A  W  W  G  A
G  O  D  E  R  A  R  E  S  P  E  C
I  W  E  S  E  K  O  R  A  T  H  R
L  F  E  S  P  E  P  X  V  L  Y  I
T  R  M  B  E  L  H  E  I  J  E  F
R  K  I  T  N  O  E  Q  O  P  G  I
E  S  A  S  T  U  T  U  R  E  M  C
V  O  Q  X  J  E  R  E  S  T  O  E
I  B  S  A  L  V  A  T  I  O  N  P
R  E  S  U  R  R  E  C  T  I  O  N
N  V  B  M  L  A  S  P  O  N  E  W
```

RESURRECTION	REDEEM	REPENT	PSALM	SACRIFICE
RIGHTTEOUS	PROPHET	SAVIOR	RIVER	SALVATION

Day 13

"And if I go and prepare a place for you, I will come back and take you to be with me that you also may be where I am."
John 14:3

"I will give you eternal life."

What this means to me?

Jesus promises to give us eternal life, a life that lasts forever with Him. How does it make you feel to know that you will always be with Jesus in heaven? Write about how you imagine heaven and what it means to you to know that you will live there forever with Jesus.

_____

_____

_____

_____

Challenge of the day:

Today, think about the promise of eternal life. Share with someone in your family what eternal life means to you and what you look forward to the most about being with Jesus forever.

Thank you prayer:

Dear Jesus, thank You for the promise of eternal life with You. I am so thankful that I will be with You forever. Please help me to remember that the best is yet to come and help me to live each day with You in my heart.
Amen.

"I will give you wisdom."

Day 14

"If any of you lacks wisdom, let him ask of God, who gives to all liberally and without reproach, and it will be given to him."
James 1:5

What this means to me?

Jesus wants to give us wisdom, which is the ability to make good choices. How does it make you feel to know that you can ask Jesus for wisdom whenever you need it? Write about a time when you made a good choice and how that choice helped you.

_____

_____

_____

_____

Challenge of the day:

Today, think about a decision you must make, big or small. Ask Jesus for wisdom to make the best choice. Afterward, share what you decided with someone in your family.

Thank you prayer:

Dear Jesus, thank You for promising to give me wisdom. I am so grateful that You want to help me make good choices. Please help me to ask for Your wisdom every day and to listen to Your guidance.
Amen.

Week 2 Recap

In week two, we focused on God's deep love for us. We discovered that God will never reject us, always defend us, and will show us compassion. Through joy, love, and eternal life, God reminds us that He has a wonderful plan for us.

Key Takeaways:
  • God will always defend us and show us kindness, even when we face hard times.
  • His love is unchanging, and He promises us eternal life through Jesus.
  • God gives us wisdom and teaches us how to live with His heart.

Family Activity Idea:
Take a walk together and talk about the ways you've experienced God's love this week.
Reflect on the promises God has given, and how they've made a difference in your family's life.

Week 3

Day 15

"For I know the plans I have for you, declares the Lord, plans for welfare and not for evil, to give you a future and a hope."
Jeremiah 29:11

"I will prosper you and bless you."

What this means to me?

God has good plans for us and wants to bless us. How does it make you feel to know that God has a plan for your future, and that He wants to give you good things? Write about a time when you saw God's blessings in your life, and how that made you feel.

_____

_____

_____

Challenge of the day:

Today, think about the good plans God has for you. Write down one thing you are thankful for that shows God's blessing in your life.

Thank you prayer:

Dear Jesus, thank You for the good plans You have for me. I am so grateful that You want to bless me and give me a bright future. Please help me to trust Your plan for my life and to always be thankful for Your blessings.
Amen.

H	E	L	O	V	E	G	J	I	J	O	Y
D	A	W	X	A	H	V	N	B	U	C	S
A	L	X	J	R	U	V	K	V	D	N	V
J	A	C	O	B	A	E	I	P	A	E	G
S	M	E	S	I	D	O	N	O	H	W	O
H	B	A	E	B	X	A	G	E	F	R	I
M	W	S	P	Y	B	Q	A	U	R	Y	Z
V	V	H	H	C	Z	J	E	S	U	S	H
C	Y	I	C	I	B	S	C	E	E	I	A
U	L	I	G	H	T	I	T	J	M	O	N
S	N	K	P	Q	K	T	P	H	K	E	O
F	J	O	T	E	L	M	E	I	L	U	J

JACOB	JESUS	JONAH	LAMB	JOY
JUDAH	KING	JOSEPH	LIGHT	LOVE

"I will give you a new heart."

Day 16

"I will give you a new heart and put a new spirit within you; I will take the heart of stone out of your flesh and give you a heart of flesh."
Ezekiel 36:26

What this means to me?

Jesus promises to give us a new heart, one that loves and follows Him. How does it make you feel to know that Jesus can change your heart to be more like His? Write about a time when you felt your heart change or when you made a choice that showed kindness and love.

_____

_____

_____

_____

Challenge of the day:

Today, ask Jesus to help you have a heart that loves others the way He loves you. Think of one way you can show love to someone today.

Thank you prayer:

Dear Jesus, thank You for giving me a new heart. I am grateful that You can change my heart and make me more like You. Please help me to love others with the new heart You've given me. Amen.

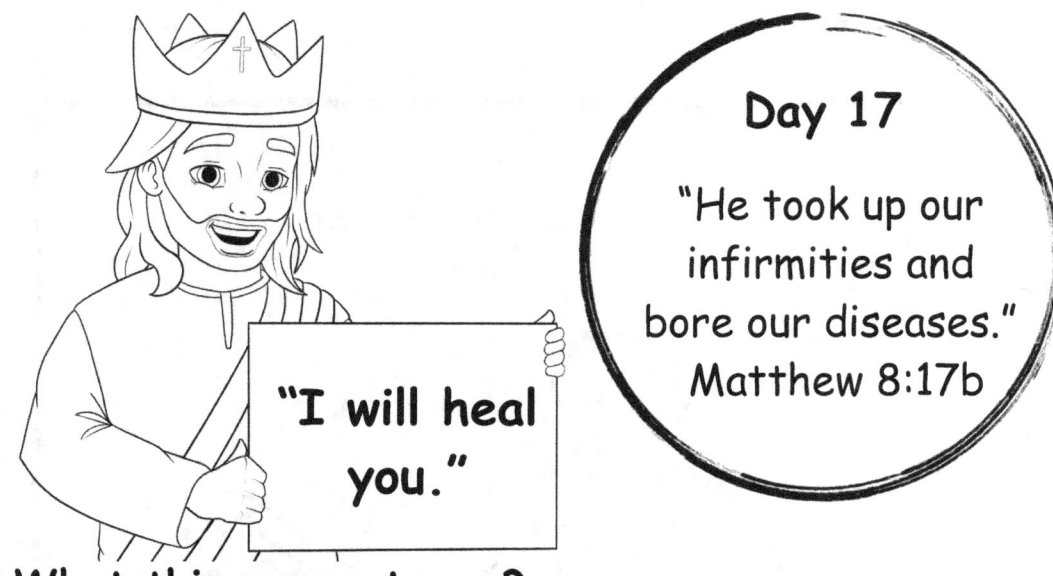

"I will heal you."

Day 17

"He took up our infirmities and bore our diseases." Matthew 8:17b

What this means to me?

Jesus cares about our pain and sickness, and He wants to heal us. How does it make you feel to know that Jesus can heal both our bodies and our hearts? Write about a time when you felt better after feeling sick or sad, and how you felt when you knew Jesus was with you.

Challenge of the day:

Today, think about someone who is sick or feeling sad. Say a prayer for them, asking Jesus to heal them and give them peace.

Thank you prayer:

Dear Jesus, thank You for caring about my pain and sickness. I'm grateful that You can heal me and make me feel better. Please help me to trust You when I need healing and to remember that You are always with me.
Amen.

Day 18

"Have I not commanded you? Be strong and courageous. Do not be afraid; do not be discouraged, for the Lord your God will be with you wherever you go."
Joshua 1:9

"I will make you strong and courageous."

What this means to me?

God promises to give us strength and courage to face any situation. How does it make you feel to know that God is always with you, helping you to be brave? Write about a time when you had to be strong or courageous, and how God helped you.

_____

_____

_____

Challenge of the day:

Think of something that makes you feel afraid or nervous. Today, ask God to help you be strong and courageous in that situation.

Thank you prayer:

Dear God, thank You for making me strong and courageous. I'm grateful that You are always with me and will help me be brave. Please help me to trust You more and to face challenges with courage.
Amen.

Day 19

"God is our refuge and strength, an ever-present help in trouble."
Psalm 46:1

"I will be your refuge and strength."

What this means to me?

God promises to be our safe place and give us strength when we are in trouble. How does it make you feel to know that God is always ready to protect and help you? Write about a time when you felt safe or strong because God was with you.

Challenge of the day:

When you face a difficult moment today, say a prayer and ask God to be your refuge and strength. Trust that He will help you.

Thank you prayer:

Dear God, thank You for being my refuge and strength. I'm so glad to know that You are always there to protect me and help me when I need it. Please help me to trust You more every day. Amen.

```
D  M  U  S  H  E  L  I  J  A  H  L
I  A  A  C  N  U  A  B  O  O  T  E
S  Q  J  D  C  H  E  X  O  D  U  S
C  R  E  A  T  I  O  N  S  O  I  V
I  G  S  V  M  J  E  R  B  D  T  E
P  B  T  I  F  A  I  T  H  W  K  S
L  I  K  D  H  D  O  V  E  I  R  T
E  S  O  O  E  K  R  P  B  N  O  H
S  I  T  W  E  G  Y  P  T  E  H  E
K  N  B  E  A  T  S  E  L  D  L  R
I  A  C  O  R  N  L  S  J  E  L  T
N  S  T  F  A  Q  T  P  Y  N  E  L
```

CREATION	EXODUS	EGYPT	EDEN	DAVID
DISCIPLES	ELIJAH	ESTHER	DOVE	FAITH

"I will comfort you when you are sad."

Day 20

"Praise be to the God and Father of our Lord Jesus Christ, the Father of compassion and the God of all comfort, who comforts us in all our troubles, so that we can comfort those in any trouble with the comfort we ourselves receive from God."
2 Corinthians 1:3-4

What this means to me?

God promises to comfort us when we feel sad or troubled. How does it make you feel to know that God is always there to bring you peace when you are sad? Write about a time when you felt comforted by God during a sad moment.

_____

_____

_____

_____

Challenge of the day:

Think of someone who might be feeling sad or troubled today. Say a prayer asking God to comfort them, just as He comforts you.

Thank you prayer:

Dear God, thank You for always comforting me when I am sad. I am grateful that You are there to bring peace and healing to my heart. Please help me to share Your comfort with others who need it.
Amen.

"Come to me, all you who are weary and burdened, and I will give you rest."
Matthew 11:28

"I will give you rest."

What this means to me?

Jesus promises to give us rest when we are tired and feeling overwhelmed. How does it make you feel to know that you can go to Jesus for rest? Write about a time when you felt tired, and how resting in Jesus gave you peace and strength.

Challenge of the day:

When you feel tired or overwhelmed today, take a moment to pray and ask Jesus to give you rest. Trust that He will give you the strength you need.

Thank you prayer:

Dear Jesus, thank You for offering me rest when I'm tired. I'm grateful that You are always there to give me peace and strength. Please help me to turn to You for rest whenever I need it.
Amen.

Week 3 Recap

We spent week three discovering how God walks with us through every moment of our
lives. God has promised to strengthen us, make us courageous, heal us, and give us
rest. We also learned how He comforts us in times of sorrow.

Key Takeaways:
   • God promises to give us strength and courage when we feel afraid.
   • He heals us from our hurts and gives us rest when we need it most.
   • In every moment, God is our refuge and comfort.

Family Activity Idea:
Encourage your child to draw a picture of a time they felt comforted by God. Share how God has helped your family feel strong during difficult times and how His promises are
always true.

Week 4

"May the God of hope fill you with all joy and peace as you trust in him, so that you may overflow with hope by the power of the Holy Spirit."
Romans 15:13

"I will give you hope."

What this means to me?

God promises to fill us with hope. How does it make you feel to know that God gives us hope, even in difficult times? Write about a time when you felt hope because of God's promises.

_____

_____

_____

_____

Challenge of the day:

Think about something you are hoping for today. Pray and ask God to fill your heart with hope, trusting that He will help you.

Thank you prayer:

Dear God, thank You for giving me hope. I am grateful that no matter what happens, I can trust in Your promises. Please help me to hold on to hope every day and share it with others. Amen.

```
H  R  V  K  L  X  I  S  A  A  C  J
B  H  O  L  Y  D  E  R  S  A  X  R
U  E  E  G  O  S  P  E  L  W  A  M
O  Y  S  F  J  A  Q  X  I  V  S  H
G  I  H  O  P  E  S  B  C  E  I  D
R  Q  Z  A  X  O  G  U  Z  Z  B  G
A  O  L  R  E  F  O  R  G  I  V  E
C  P  E  D  O  E  D  N  Q  J  U  N
E  C  A  R  V  X  Z  I  A  S  T  E
Z  T  R  H  I  F  U  S  F  E  G  S
T  K  S  J  H  E  A  V  E  N  E  I
C  N  I  Z  C  V  W  Q  T  F  A  S
```

FORGIVE	GOD	GENESIS	HOPE	GRACE
HEAVEN	HOLY	GOSPEL	ISAAC	ISRAEL

"I will rescue you from danger."

Day 23

"The righteous cry out, and the Lord hears them; he delivers them from all their troubles."
Psalm 34:17

What this means to me?

God promises to rescue us from danger and troubles. How does it make you feel to know that God is always ready to help and protect you? Write about a time when you felt rescued or protected by God.

Challenge of the day:

Think about someone who may be facing danger or a difficult situation today. Pray for God to protect them and rescue them from trouble.

Thank you prayer:

Dear God, thank You for rescuing me from danger and protecting me. I am so thankful that I can trust You to keep me safe. Please help me to trust in Your protection every day. Amen.

"I will protect you with my angels."

Day 24

"For he will command his angels concerning you to guard you in all your ways;"
Psalm 91:11

What this means to me?

God promises to send His angels to protect us. How does it make you feel to know that God has angels watching over you? Write about a time when you felt God's protection or safety and imagine His angels surrounding you.

_____

_____

_____

Challenge of the day:

Think of someone who needs protection today, like a friend or family member. Pray and ask God to send His angels to watch over them and keep them safe.

Thank you prayer:

Dear God, thank You for sending Your angels to protect me. I'm so grateful that You keep me safe from harm. Please help me to trust in Your protection every day, knowing that Your angels are with me.

Amen.

"I will provide for all your needs."

Day 25

"And my God will meet all your needs according to the riches of his glory in Christ Jesus."
Philippians 4:19

What this means to me?

God promises to take care of everything you need. How does it make you feel knowing that God will always provide for you? Write about something you have prayed for and how God provided for you in that situation.

Challenge of the day:

Think of one need you have today (like food, clothes, or even something smaller). Thank God for meeting that need and trust that He will continue to provide for you.

Thank you prayer:

Dear God, thank You for always providing for me and taking care of my needs. Help me to trust You more and remember that You will never leave me without what I need.
Amen.

"I will make your path straight."

Day 26

"Trust in the Lord with all your heart and lean not on your own understanding; in all your ways submit to him, and he will make your paths straight."
Proverbs 3:5-6

What this means to me?

God promises to guide you and help you make good choices. When you trust Him and follow His ways, He will lead you on the right path. Write about a time when you trusted God and felt His guidance in your life.

_____

_____

_____

_____

Challenge of the day:

Think of a decision you need to make. Pray and ask God for guidance, trusting that He will lead you in the right direction.

Thank you prayer:

Dear God, thank You for always guiding me and helping me make the right choices. Help me to trust You with all my heart and follow Your path for my life.
Amen.

```
E  A  P  O  S  T  L  E  M  E  R  L
V  A  A  C  N  U  A  B  R  E  A  D
A  Q  J  A  C  H  G  T  O  U  N  A
C  C  O  M  M  A  N  D  S  O  I  T
A  H  S  E  M  J  I  R  B  D  T  N
P  U  T  C  M  A  S  A  A  W  K  A
A  R  K  R  H  C  S  P  P  I  R  N
M  C  O  O  E  K  E  B  I  B  L  E
P  H  T  W  B  E  L  L  S  D  H  V
K  N  B  E  A  T  B  E  T  Y  L  O
I  A  N  G  E  L  L  S  L  L  L  C
N  S  T  E  C  R  O  S  S  R  E  L
```

ANGEL   APOSTLE   COVENANT   BIBLE   BLESSING

BREAD   CHURCH   COMMAND   ARK   CROSS

"I will never forget you."

Day 27

"Remember these things, Jacob, for Israel is my servant. I have made you; you are my servant; Israel, I will not forget you."
Isaiah 44:21

What this means to me?

God promises that He will never forget you. No matter what happens, He always remembers you and cares for you. Write about a time when you felt God's love and presence, knowing that He will never forget you.

_____

_____

_____

_____

Challenge of the day:

Take a moment today to think about all the ways God has shown His love for you. Thank Him for never forgetting you, even when things are hard.

Thank you prayer:

Dear God, thank You for always remembering me and never forgetting me. I am so thankful for Your love and care. Help me to trust in You always, knowing that You will never leave me. Amen.

Day 28

"The Lord is my light and my salvation whom shall I fear? The Lord is the stronghold of my life of whom shall I be afraid?"
Psalm 27:1

"I will be your light."

What this means to me?

God promises to be your light, shining in the darkness and guiding you. How does it feel to know that God will always be there to light your way? Write about a time when you felt God's light leading you in the right direction.

_____

_____

_____

Challenge of the day:

Think of a situation where you feel confused or afraid. Pray and ask God to be your light in that situation and help you find your way.

Thank you prayer:

Dear God, thank You for being my light and for guiding me through every dark moment. Help me to trust You more and remember that You are always with me, shining Your light. Amen.

"I will give you My Holy Spirit to guide you."

Day 29

"But the Advocate, the Holy Spirit, whom the Father will send in my name, will teach you all things and will remind you of everything I have said to you."
John 14:26

What this means to me?

God promises to send His Holy Spirit to help guide you, teach you, and remind you of His words. How does it feel to know that the Holy Spirit is always with you, helping you make the right choices? Write about a time when you felt the Holy Spirit guiding you.

Challenge of the day:

Today, pray and ask the Holy Spirit to guide you. Think of a decision you need to make and ask for His wisdom in that situation.

Thank you prayer:

Dear God, thank You for sending Your Holy Spirit to guide me and teach me. Help me to listen to Your Spirit and follow Your guidance every day.
Amen.

I will never lie to you; I always do what I promise. You can count on Me!

Day 30

Let us hold fast the confession of our hope without wavering, for He who promised is faithful.
Hebrews 10:23

What this means to me?

Jesus always tells the truth and keeps His promises. How does it make you feel to know you can trust Him no matter what? Write about a time when someone kept a promise to you and how it made you feel.

Challenge of the day:

Think of one promise Jesus makes in the Bible (like He will always love you or be with you). Say it out loud to yourself today and share it with someone in your family.

Thank you prayer:

Dear Jesus, thank You for always keeping Your promises and for never lying. Help me to trust You more each day and to remember that I can always count on You.
Amen

Week 4 Recap

In the final week, we focused on God's ongoing faithfulness. From providing for our needs to be our light and guiding us, God has shown us that He is always there to lead and protect us. He has given us His Holy Spirit to walk with us every day.

Key Takeaways:
  • God promises to provide for us and make our paths straight.
  • He will never forget us and is always our light in dark times.
  • We have the Holy Spirit to help us live in God's truth.

Family Activity Idea:
Before finishing the devotional, gather as a family and reflect on all the promises you've learned about. Thank God for His faithfulness, and pray together for His continued
guidance in your lives.

Notes:

I'm sorry for:

Help me with:

I'm grateful for:

Notes:

I'm sorry for:

Help me with:

I'm grateful for:

Notes:

I'm sorry for:

Help me with:

I'm grateful for:

Notes:

I'm sorry for:

Help me with:

I'm grateful for:

Notes:

I'm sorry for:

Help me with:

I'm grateful for:

Notes:

I'm sorry for:

Help me with:

I'm grateful for:

Notes:

I'm sorry for:

Help me with:

I'm grateful for:

Notes:

I'm sorry for:

Help me with:

I'm grateful for:

Notes:

I'm sorry for:

Help me with:

I'm grateful for: